For our husbands, Jason and Allen,
who have shown us what it means
to truly love us "in sickness and in health".
Thank you for all your
encouragement and support.

## A Word from Vicki (the author)

A few years ago, I decided to concentrate on the psalms during my quiet times with God, immersing myself in just one psalm each day. I took the time to read them in several translations and to understand them on a heart level, whilst applying them to my own life. Once I had spent time meditating on them, I penned a prayer based on each psalm.

I found these prayers to be such a personal blessing and believed these should not be kept to myself, but something to be shared with others. I did this mostly through Facebook and received some good feedback. Several people commented that they would be great in a book. This book, "Pause in God's Presence: Praying the Psalms Volume 1 Psalms 1-75" and its companion book, "Pause in God's presence: Praying the Psalms Volume 2: Psalms 76-150" is the result of the time I spent alone in psalms and the encouragement I received from others.

I have self-published a previous book, "Praying Through Proverbs" which included colour photos, but this time I wanted to do something different. It was some months back I discovered my friend, Lisa, from church, had a gift for drawing and she shared her artwork on social media. I approached her to see if she would be happy to illustrate my prayers with her black and white illustrations. I don't think she initially realised the magnitude of the task – I wanted one illustration per prayer, which amounted to over 150 (as I had broken down Psalm 119 into several prayers)!

However, she agreed and has spent many hours creating these beautiful illustrations. She will be sharing with you a bit of her story in the next section.

When you read the Book of Psalms in the Bible, you will come across the word "Selah" or "Interlude". It appears seventy-one times in the psalms and many commentators believe it is a musical term and means "to pause or reflect". This is what I did as I read through the psalms, I would pause, reflect, and meditate on what I read. One of the Bible translations I used was The Passion Translation and instead of the word 'Selah', they used the term, 'Pause in his presence' which gave me the title for this book. What a joy and privilege it is to take time to pause and rest in God's presence and allow him to minister to our hearts, minds, and souls.

*Vicki*

## A Word from Lisa (the illustrator)

I have always loved reading the Psalms and I tend to meditate on one a day. When Vicki approached me, I had just found out I had breast cancer and would need an operation and chemotherapy for 6 months. I have always worked full-time, loving my job as a nursery manager which I have done for eighteen years.

Before Vicki spoke to me, I had prayed to God asking him how he could use me now I couldn't work and would be at home isolating for a year. I felt very disheartened.

One day during prayer I heard him say very clearly, "Use your talents". I didn't know what to make of that but then my eyes fell on my prayer journal which was filled with doodles and drawings, and I realised that I now had the time to do my artwork (something I never had the time to do before).

My husband suggested I start to share my pictures on social media. To my utter surprise and delight, it really took off and before I knew it, I had made many Christian friends from all over the world who messaged me daily to say how my pictures inspired and helped them with God's Word.

When Vicki asked me to illustrate her book, I was beyond honoured and very excited. I knew God had his hand in it. Vicki would send me her beautiful psalm reflection which I would meditate and pray over and ask for help and guidance on how to illustrate it. Most times God would put a picture in my head, and I would prayerfully draw that image. The process was very spiritual and uplifting and distracted me from the effects of the chemotherapy. I honestly felt the Holy Spirit took over when I drew, and I felt so thoroughly blessed by God and looked after during this new phase in my life. I felt so close to God whilst I drew, and I pray you will be able to draw close to him too as you colour in the pictures.

God always has a good plan for our lives, and He has been so faithful. Even the cancer which should have caused grief led me to an unexpected year of pure joy and happiness and I am so thankful for the year I have had.

*Lisa*

# How To Use This Book

"Pause in God's Presence" is a short meditative book. The aim of the book is to help you engage with the psalms and meditate and reflect on them prayerfully and mindfully. My written prayer based on each psalm may lead you into your own prayer based on that psalm. One way of using this book would be to first open your own Bible and read the psalm (or read it online) and then go on to read the accompanying prayer.

I have included Lisa's illustrations as an aid to help with your reflections and meditations on God's Word. There is the option for those of you who enjoy mindful colouring to colour in the illustrations should you wish to. You can use the illustrations as another way to connect with the psalm and meditate and reflect on it, or you can reflect on the psalm as you colour it in.

My desire is that this book will help you to take time during the day to pause in God's presence.

We lead such busy, full lives and so often we can forget to include God in our day. This is a book that will help people to connect or reconnect with God for a few moments. Now, more than ever, people need that connection with God, and I believe the recent pandemic has highlighted our need for connection and our need to stop and rest in our day.

I know over the last few years there has also been a return to Christian mindfulness and the realisation, especially in my life, that our service to God needs to overflow from our relationship with him. I believe my book will be a tool to help you to do this.

There is now also a greater understanding and awareness of mental wellbeing, and the need to care for our wellbeing. This book is one way of helping people in this area. Spending time in the psalms is a great way of helping us express our emotions in a healthy way. Reading the psalms also helps to strengthen our spiritual wellbeing.

The language I have used in my prayers is, I believe, honest and relevant, and I believe can help people to express themselves before God in their own words or by making the words of my prayers their own.

# Psalm 1

*Lord God,*

Thank you for your Word. I delight in meditating on it as I go about my day and as I fall asleep at night. Thank you for all the wisdom found within the pages of your book. As you reveal your truth to me in your Word, may I follow your path for my life. Thank you for watching over me. Lead me I pray.

*Amen.*

I delight in
your Word

# Psalm 2

*Lord God,*

Thank you that you are Sovereign and you reign from on high. Help me to willingly submit to your will for my life. May I always remember you want the best for me and will never ask something of me which is not for my good.

*Amen.*

I submit to you,
Lord

# Psalm 3

*Lord God,*

There are times in my life when I struggle, when my fears, worries and doubts take over, when I am overwhelmed by life. These things can all disturb my nights and stop me sleeping in peace. When I feel this way help me to remember you are with me. I can cry out to you and you will hear because you are right beside me. As I settle down for the night may you enfold me in your love and peace so I may sleep well and wake refreshed, ready to face the new day.

*Amen.*

You are with me

# Psalm 4

*Lord God,*

As I lay down to sleep this night I reflect over my day. I remember with a grateful heart how you have been present in the things I have done and I give thanks to you again. But I also search my heart and remember the times when I have sinned against you, when I have ignored you, and done the things I have wanted to. When I have done and said things which have hurt you. For those things I am sorry now and ask for your forgiveness. In confessing them, I once again feel the peace and joy only you can bring. Because of you I can now lie down in peace and sleep.

*Amen.*

I lie down in peace and sleep

# Psalm 5

*Lord God,*

Thank you that in your grace you welcome me into your presence. Thank you so much for always hearing me and paying attention to me. Help me to be still as I come into your presence and help me to wait expectantly to hear your voice. When I come with an attitude of expectation you never disappoint. As you bend your ear to listen to me, may I do the same.

*Amen.*

You bend
your ear
to me

# Psalm 6

*Lord God,*

Thank you that I can always be totally honest with you. I can tell you how I am feeling and the struggles I am facing. You never dismiss my feelings or ignore them. Thank you for hearing my cries. Help me to be patient as I wait for your answer.

*Amen.*

You hear my cry for help

# Psalm 7

*Lord God,*

*Thank you for seeing the real me, who I am on the inside. You see and know my thoughts, my emotions, my passions, desires, fears, worries, struggles and motives. Would you plant in me a deep desire to know and follow you God.*

*Amen.*

Plant in me
a desire to
know and
follow you

# Psalm 8

*Lord God,*

I praise you for the wonder of creation. Everything you created is amazing. Not only are you the creator of all things, you also created me, and because you did, I am always on your mind. This is such a precious thought to me! Thank you, God.

*Amen.*

I praise you for the wonder of creation

# Psalm 9

*Lord God,*

May my heart be one of praise for who you are and all you mean to me. I praise you because you are my refuge, my safe place and one who is worthy of my trust. You will never abandon me. Would you also give me the boldness to share the wonder of you with others.

*Amen.*

You will
never
abandon
me

# Psalm 10

*Lord God,*

I pray on behalf of my brothers and sisters in Christ who face such terrible persecution. Would you please give them the courage and strength to keep following you whatever the cost. As they do so, may they experience your love, comfort and presence in amazing ways.

*Amen.*

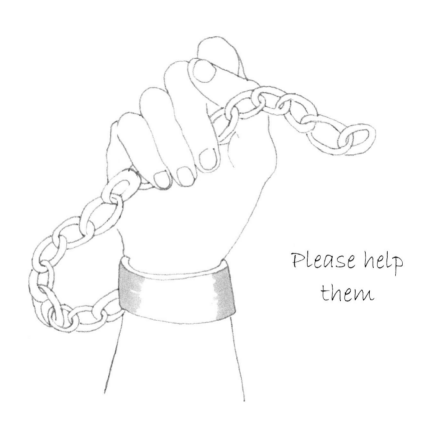

Please help them

# Psalm 11

*Lord God,*

Help me to remember to come to you first with my problems. Help me to keep trusting you and to commit my worries to you rather than looking to human wisdom for help. Thank you that no matter how it may appear, you still rule and you are in control.

*Amen.*

# Psalm 12

*Lord God,*

Your promises and word is pure. I can completely trust what you say. I keep believing in and holding onto your promises in your Word because you are faithful. Your word is true. As I read your word may I get to know you and your word better. May your words become such a strong part of me, that all I say and the way I say them all be pleasing to you.

*Amen.*

I trust in your word

# Psalm 13

*Lord God,*

How long before you answer my prayers? How long will I have to wait for you to act? How long will this season last? Even so, I choose to trust in your unfailing love. I choose to rejoice and praise you because you are good.

*Amen.*

Please
answer
my
prayer

# Psalm 14

*Lord God,*

Help me to be wise this day. I need your wisdom in every aspect of my life. Thank you for generously giving me your wisdom. Wisdom is based on seeking you and being obedient to your will. May I always seek to please you. Thank you for your promise to be with me always.

*Amen.*

Please help me
to be wise
today

# Psalm 15

*Lord God,*

Thank you that I can come before your throne with confidence not in myself, but because of what Jesus has done for me. Thank you that he makes me righteous. By the help of the Holy Spirit may I live out the godly nature you have planted within me.

*Amen.*

I come
before your
throne

# Psalm 16

Lord God,

You are the source of my confidence and my reason for contentment. You have blessed me in so many ways. You are always with me, you are my refuge and your presence brings me joy. Thank you that because you are with me, I will not be shaken. Thank you that not even death can separate me from you.

*Amen.*

You have blessed me in so
many ways

# Psalm 17

*Lord God,*

Thank you that I can have confidence in knowing you pay attention to my cry and you will answer me. Thank you that I am precious to you. Thank you for your protection and for guiding me as the apple of your eye. Thank you for hiding me in the shadow of your wings.

*Amen.*

Thank you for
hiding me in
your wings

# Psalm 18

*Lord God,*

I'm in a season right now where things seem less than perfect. Life is hard and I am struggling. Keep me strong in my faith and keep me following your way because I know you are perfect. You can be trusted and I know every one of your promises will prove true. May your promises and your word settle deep in my heart so that I have these to cling to when everything else says differently.

*Amen.*

May your
promises
settle deep
in my heart

# Psalm 19

*Lord God,*

I know there are times when I have spoken words of anger, bitterness, unforgiveness, envy etc. The moment I've spoken them I am sorry and know I've been wrong. Forgive me, Lord. By your Spirit would you help me to speak words of life and love, words which please you and build others up. Help me to be deliberate about what I allow into my mind, may they be things which are pleasing and honouring to you. When I recognise a thought, which is not of you, help me to reject it and replace it with thoughts which are pure and acceptable to you.

*Amen.*

Forgive me,
Lord

# Psalm 20

*Lord God,*

I believe there are certain desires that you have placed in my heart. I believe they are your will for me. They may be buried deep in my heart but they are still there, sown and planted by you. I know Lord that seeds take time to grow, help me to be patient and wait for your timing. Would you grow that which you have planted in me so I can fulfil your purposes for me. In faith I say, thank you, Lord.

*Amen.*

You plant seeds in my heart

# Psalm 21

*Lord God,*

Thank you for every blessing in my life. All that I have comes from you. Most of all, I thank you for your presence in my life. I trust you because you have always promised to be with me. You have never left me on my own and you never will. I can have a confident trust in you because you are God and you keep all your promises. You are in control of everything that happens. Because you are with me, I will never be shaken.

*Amen.*

# Psalm 22

*Lord God,*

My pain is almost too much to bear. It feels like you have turned your back on me. It feels like you've abandoned me. You don't hear me cry or see my tears. Yet, you Jesus know what it means to suffer and feel abandoned by God and you know my pain. God, you alone can help me. I know you don't look the other way when I am in pain. You are with me in my pain even when it doesn't feel like it. I will praise you and I will find you.

*Amen.*

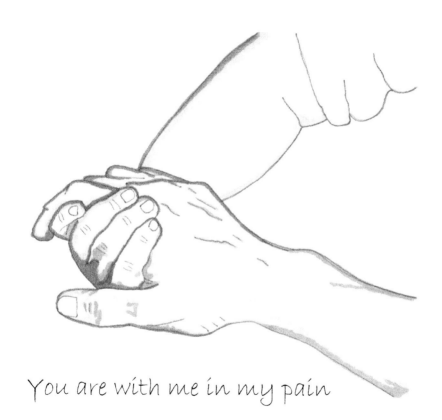

You are with me in my pain

# Psalm 23

*Lord Jesus,*

Thank you for being the good shepherd of my life. Thank you that because of you, I have all that I need. Thank you for the times you have led me to places of quiet and rest in where you have refreshed and restored me. Even when I have walked through dark and difficult times your comforting presence is still with me. Thank you for always being with me. My cup overflows with every blessing from you. I know your goodness, grace and mercy pursues me all the days of my life. I look forward to the day I will dwell at home with you forever. May I always be an obedient sheep who willingly follows the lead of my shepherd.

*Amen.*

You are my Good Shepherd

# Psalm 24

*Lord Jesus,*

You are my Saviour, you are the King of Glory and the Lord of Heaven's Armies. Only you are worthy of my worship. I praise you that you have made me righteous so I can come into God's presence. Help me to come with an attitude which says 'I'm willing to wait quietly before you, to be still and listen for your voice.'

*Amen.*

I will wait quietly before you

# Psalm 25

*Lord God,*

I have tightly wrapped my heart around yours. With all my heart I wait on you and your purposes. I know there is a private place reserved for me and those like me who long to know you more intimately and to be near you. A place where you reveal the secrets of your word to me. Then, take me by the hand and teach me to understand your ways. Show me your ways and purposes because I hope and trust in you.

*Amen.*

Reveal the secrets of your word to me

# Psalm 26

*Lord God,*

I want to live a life of integrity, to be wholly devoted to you. You know my heart better than I do myself. Would you examine my motives and my heart. Reveal to me those things which are of value, glorifying to you and remove the dross, that which hinders my devotion to you. When you have tested me, may I come out as gold.

*Amen.*

You know
my heart

# Psalm 27

Lord God,

My heart longs for you, to be always in your presence. You are my hiding place. My confidence and my hope is in you.

*Amen.*

You are my
hiding
place

# Psalm 28

*Lord God,*

I cry out to you for help. Won't you hear my cry? I need to hear your voice. I need your protection. I need that inner strength which only you can give me. Without it I will fall. I'm not strong enough to withstand the assaults that are coming against me. Today in my weakness, will you carry me in your arms because right now I just can't take one more step. Thank you, Lord.

*Amen.*

Lord, carry
me in your
arms

# Psalm 29

*Lord God,*

Your name is glorious. Your voice is powerful and majestic. You reign forever. I'm struggling in the storm right now. Help me to remember you are God in the thunderstorm. You are mightier than the storm. I ask that you would bless me with your strength and your peace in the midst of this storm.

*Amen.*

You are mightier than the storm

# Psalm 30

Lord God,

There seems to be no end to the dark night of my soul, no end to my deepest pains which only you really know about. But I know you alone can turn my deepest pain into deepest joy. This dark night will not last forever and the day will come when I will praise you for all eternity.

Amen.

You turn my pain to joy

# Psalm 31

Lord God,

Thank you that my future is in your hands. What a reassuring thought that is! I entrust my whole being to you. You are my safe place. My hope is in you alone. It is this hope which gives me strength and courage to face the day.

Amen.

My future is in your hands

# Psalm 32

*Lord God,*

What joy, blessing and freedom there is in your forgiveness. Thank you that when I confess my sins you promise to forgive me and wipe my slate clean. When I am unrepentant, I distance myself from you. But when I choose to live in obedience, I am close to you and sense you watching over me, guiding me on the best pathway for my life. Thank you, Lord.

*Amen.*

You guide me on the best pathway

# Psalm 33

Lord God,

You have placed a new song of praise on my lips. You have filled my heart with joy. I have so many reasons to praise you – you have chosen me to belong to you and you love me with an unfailing love. I trust in your word, there is power in your word. Your strength and might surpasses all others. Thank you for watching over me. Thank you that your plans for me can never be shaken.

*Amen.*

You have placed a
song on my lips

# Psalm 34

*Lord God,*

May my praise of you ever be on my lips. May my face be radiant with the joy of the Lord so others will see you are good. When my heart is broken and my spirit is crushed because of the troubles I face, you come close to me and you comfort me as only you know how. Whatever is happening in my life, you are all I need. And that is why I praise you.

*Amen.*

May my
face be
radiant
with the joy
of the Lord

# Psalm 35

*Lord God,*

No one can compare with you. Stay close to me and hear my prayer. I am in pain and distress, hurt by those who falsely accuse me, who lie about me, who abuse me, who say all manner of evil things to me to bring me down. Put a guard over my mouth, so I won't retaliate or return like for like. I look to you to defend me, to fight for me. You are my Saviour and I rejoice in your salvation.

*Amen.*

I look to you to
defend me

# Psalm 36

*Lord God,*

How amazing, unlimited, all-encompassing is your love to me. You overwhelm me with your love. You are the fountain of life-giving water, only you can quench my thirst, only you can satisfy the hunger in my soul.

*Amen.*

You are the fountain
of life-giving water

# Psalm 37

Lord God,

I delight in you and I know you delight in every detail of my life. I entrust my life to you. Please direct my steps because my heart longs to do your will. Hold my hand so that even when I trip I will not fall.

*Amen.*

Please direct
my steps

# Psalm 38

*Lord God,*

I've held on to my sin and it's making me ill - physically, mentally and spiritually. But now I'm confessing it. I'm so deeply sorry. Please show me mercy God and forgive me. My sin caused a barrier between us. Please restore me, don't abandon me. Draw close to me and help me I pray.

*Amen.*

Please show me mercy
and forgiveness

# Psalm 39

*Lord God,*

When I'm going through a difficult time it can feel so long and unending. Help me to remember my time here on earth is fleeting and temporary. Remind me I am just travelling through and one day I will enjoy my permanent home with you in heaven. As I journey help me to remember my hope and confident expectation is in you.

*Amen.*

Heaven – my permanent home

# Psalm 40

*Lord God,*

My troubles are surrounding me, I can see no way out. There is no light at the end of this long, dark tunnel. Won't you rescue me? Won't you help me? I know I am always in your thoughts, that you are ever mindful of me. I've been in this place before - in the deep, dark pit, sinking further into the mire, unable to save myself. You rescued me then, you gently lifted me out, set me on solid ground and enabled me to stand. You've done it before and I know you will do it again. My trust and my confidence are in you.

*Amen.*

Please rescue me

# Psalm 41

*Lord God,*

There have been times in my life when I've felt so alone, when even those closest to me have misunderstood me, and it's brought me so much pain. But I'm so grateful to know you as my true friend, you stand with me no matter what. You have never deserted me. Thank you I can call you friend and that you call me friend.

*Amen.*

You have never
deserted me

# Psalm 42

*Lord God,*

I am in deep despair, my heart is broken, I am discouraged and miserable. I can't stop my tears from flowing, yet I don't really know why. I can't explain it even to myself. There is this overwhelming sadness of spirit which is threatening to drown me. And yet, deep calls out to deep, you are right there with me and I know you will break through for me, just as you have before. I will choose to praise you. I will choose to sing songs to you even whilst I am in this dark place. For you are my Saviour and my God.

*Amen.*

Even in my tears, I will praise you

# Psalm 43

*Lord God,*

Thank you for being my safe haven. In you is my security. Your truth is the only truth I want to live by. When I can't trust my own feelings, I can trust in your word, in the truth which is always unchanging. Thank you for your light in the darkness. The darkness can never extinguish your light. Your truth and your light guide me each day.

*Amen.*

Thank you for your light

# Psalm 44

*Lord God,*

When I am in the trial and the difficulties of life, would you help me to remember to do two things. First, to keep trusting in you because you are trustworthy and you will bring me through victorious. Secondly, to look back over my past experiences and those of other men and women who have followed you and remember that just as you have always been faithful and loving, so you will continue to be so.

*Amen.*

I look back and remember
your faithfulness

# Psalm 45

*Lord God,*

*You have chosen me to be your royal daughter. That is who I am - a daughter of the King. Help me to live out of the reality of my identity. Not only that, you have chosen me to be the bride of Christ. I choose to honour him as my husband and Lord. I forsake all other loves and live devoted to him.*

*Amen.*

I am your royal child

# Psalm 46

Lord God,

Thank you that in the midst of the chaos and uncertainty you are right there with me. I trust you. Instead of wanting to be in control would you help me please to let go and surrender it all into your hands. Help me to remember you alone are God and everything is under your control so I have nothing to fear.

Amen.

Everything is
under your
control

# Psalm 47

*Lord God,*

Most High, Almighty One, awesome in power, Great King of heaven and earth. I bring my joyful praise to you. I clap my hands and shout for joy and sing praises to your name. Thank you for sending your son, Jesus, to earth so I would come to know you. And now Jesus is seated at your right hand as King of Kings. You reign forever and ever, and I will sing your praises.

*Amen.*

I bring you
my joyful praise

# Psalm 48

*Lord God,*

My God. How great you are. No one can compare with you and none can stand against you. I am a citizen of your heavenly kingdom and you are my God and my King. I meditate on your unfailing love for me, on your goodness and kindness to me. One day I will worship you face to face. But until that day comes, I will continue to speak and sing of your greatness and your love.

*Amen.*

You are my God and King

# Psalm 49

Lord God,

I have nothing to fear in this life or the next because you have redeemed me through the precious blood of your dear son, Jesus Christ. Help me to live today with eternity in view, storing up treasure in heaven. May I be more concerned with becoming more like Jesus than with gaining earthly treasure which counts for nothing.

Amen.

Treasure in heaven

# Psalm 50

*Lord God,*

Too often have I just gone through the motions of following you, of doing the "right" thing because that's what is expected of me. But this counts for nothing if my heart is not in it. Today I'm offering you my thankful heart, so that everything I do springs from a heart of gratitude. Then all I do will be pleasing to you.

*Amen.*

# Heart of Gratitude

# Psalm 51

*Lord God,*

My sin has left me broken. I lay my heart open before you and confess my desire to do my own will was more important to me than following your will. Only you can forgive me and make me whole. Please restore me and give me a brand-new heart, one that is ready and willing to do your will.

*Amen.*

I lay my heart open before you

# Psalm 52

*Lord God,*

I trust in your unfailing love. You are my rescuer and my Saviour. My hope is in you. Time and again you have proved I can depend on you. I am like an olive tree which flourishes in your presence. May my roots grow down deep in you so that my faith in you will grow stronger and my love for you will grow deeper. As this happens my heart will overflow with thanks and praise.

*Amen.*

Like an olive tree I flourish in your presence

# Psalm 53

*Lord God,*

I may not be wise in the eyes of the world, but I know that when I ask you for your wisdom you generously give it to me. I seek you God because I know how much I need you. I need your wisdom every moment of every day. I can't live my life without you. Thank you that as my heart seeks you, I will find you.

*Amen.*

I need your wisdom every moment

# Psalm 54

*Lord God,*

When I go through difficult times I can feel so alone. Those I thought would be there for me have let me down. But you, God, are good. I trust in your mighty name and in your faithfulness. Help me to hold on to your promises. You are the one who sustains me. And so, I choose right now to bring you my sacrifice of praise.

*Amen.*

I am holding onto your

PROMISES

# Psalm 55

*Lord God,*

I'm breaking under the weight of the burdens I'm carrying. Burdens you've not asked me to bear on my own. So today, I'm piling them onto your shoulders because yours are broad and strong. Thank you for being the One who sustains me, upholds me and cares for me.

*Amen.*

I am breaking
under the
weight of
my burdens

# Psalm 56

*Lord God,*

Whatever is happening in my life, I choose to put my trust in you and in your promises. My confidence is in you. My courage comes from you. I have no need to fear the present or the future because you are with me.

*Amen.*

My confidence is in you

# Psalm 57

*Lord God,*

In the middle of this spiritual battle in which Satan is prowling, seeking to devour me, I cry out to you, the Mighty God. Instead of trying to hide and isolate myself I come to you and ask that you protect me and keep me safe under the shadow of your wings. I trust in you and your purposes for me. My confidence is in you alone. This is why I am able to sing your praises and lift you high.

*Amen.*

Protect me
and keep me safe

# Psalm 58

Lord God,

May all I do and say be characterised by truth and justice. Help me to love others and treat them as you do. I see injustice around me and how people are treated unfairly. I know how this deeply saddens you. You are a just God and in your time, you will judge with justice and righteousness.

Amen.

You judge with justice and righteousness

# Psalm 59

*Lord God,*

I recognise my weakness and my frailty, but you, God, are my strength, and as I wait on you, you give me your strength. All I am able to do is because of your power working in me. *Thank you* when I depend on you to work through me all the praise and glory goes to you, O Mighty God.

*Amen.*

God, you are my strength

# Psalm 60

Lord God,

I run to you, because you are my banner. You are my powerful defender, my refuge and my help. You are the source of my confidence. You are the one who makes a way for me and I thank you for the constancy of your presence with me.

Amen.

I run to you,
Lord

# Psalm 61

*Lord God,*

Please hear my heart's cry. I don't feel you close right now. Life has me feeling overwhelmed. My poor physical health has weakened me and left me feeling helpless. Yet I know I can find shelter under your wings. I know you have given me your Holy Spirit and he has made his home in me. In your unfailing love and faithfulness won't you please watch over me and guard me.

*Amen.*

Please watch over me and guide me

# Psalm 62

*Lord God,*

My Saviour, my strong tower and my rock. I run to you because you are my refuge. My confidence, trust and hope are in you and I will not be shaken. I sit in the quiet and the stillness, surrendering myself to you. My whole being waits on you, knowing at just the right time you will act.

*Amen.*

You are my refuge

# Psalm 63

*Lord God,*

Only you can satisfy the hunger in my soul, only you can quench my thirsty soul with your life-giving water. And so, I daily feed on your word and drink from your stream of living water. I cling to you because you mean so much to me, and as I cling to you, I sense your right hand holding fast to me.

*Amen.*

Only you can quench
my thirst

# Psalm 64

*Lord God,*

It's been said, 'Sticks and stones may break my bones, but words will never hurt me.' But this just isn't true. Things people have said to me have caused me intense pain. Their words have cut me to the core. They have left deep wounds. Today, I come to you, God and ask you would heal those wounds. I take refuge in you. I choose to focus on the words you speak over me, when you tell me that you love me, that you delight in me and that I am your treasured possession. Thank you there is healing in your words - they are a balm to my soul.

*Amen.*

Please heal
my deep wounds

# Psalm 65

*Lord God,*

I stand in awe of you. Creation provides evidence of your presence, your power, and your provision. All creation is under your authority. Yet, at the same time, you still show me that you care for me. You have chosen me and given me access to yourself. What joy is found in knowing not only do you hear my prayers but you answer them too. My heart overflows with joy and praise.

*Amen.*

All creation is
under your
authority

# Psalm 66

*Lord God,*

I bring my praise to you as I remember your faithfulness and your never-failing love for me. You have always been good to me. Even the trials you have allowed me to go through have been for my good. They have been to test and refine me, to change me into the image of your son, Jesus. Thank you that my life is in your hands and that you keep me faithfully following you. There is no place I'd rather be.

*Amen.*

Even tests and trials
are for my good

# Psalm 67

*Lord God,*

My heart overflows with praise to you for all the many blessings you have poured out on me. I don't deserve anything, yet in your grace and mercy you love to give me good gifts. I love that when you turn your face to me, you smile at me. May my life, as your child, always bring you joy. Help me to bless others as you have blessed me.

*Amen.*

Help me to bless others as you have
blessed me

# Psalm 68

*Lord God,*

You are mighty and majestic in power. You rule from on high. You are the Almighty King and yet you have shown your care for me again and again. You have rescued me and saved me from death. You are compassionate to me and give me all I need. I thank you that you carry me in your arms and that day after day you shoulder my burdens. What joy I have found in just being in your presence, thank you, God.

*Amen.*

I thank you that
you carry me in
your arms

# Psalm 69

*Lord God,*

My suffering and my pain is more than I can bear. It has broken me. No one understands and I feel like I'm drowning in deep waters. Won't you lift me out of them and enable me to stand? My eyes are swollen from all my tears and I'm exhausted from crying. You know what it means to suffer. You've experienced what real pain is. I know you understand and care. Draw close to me. Hear my prayer. Answer my cry and comfort me. I wait with confident expectation.

*Amen.*

My suffering
and pain has
broken me

# Psalm 70

Lord God,

I am weak and helpless. I so need you. Please remember me and come quickly to my aid because you are my helper and my Saviour. I seek you as my first priority in life. My heart overflows with joy when I remember all that you are and all you have done for me, for you are a great God.

*Amen.*

You have cared
for me since I
was in my
mother's
womb

# Psalm 71

*Lord God,*

You have cared for me since I was in my mother's womb. You have been with me all my life. I have trusted you from when I was very young. You have been my teacher and my guide. You continue to care for me through my adult years. You are the rock on which I stand. You are the source of my confidence and my hope. My life is an example to those around me. May I never stop telling of your faithfulness and your goodness from this generation to the next.

*Amen.*

My heart
overflows
with joy

# Psalm 72

*Lord Jesus,*

I worship and honour you as King of Kings. You alone are worthy of my praise. You are a just and righteous King, defender of the poor, the weak and those who are oppressed. Each one is precious to you. You will reign forever and one day all peoples will bow before you. I willingly submit to you and your authority over me. I give my life in service to you.

*Amen.*

You alone are
worthy of my
praise

# Psalm 73

*Lord God,*

You are a good God and you are good to me. Sometimes, when I look around me, I can forget this. So, I draw near to you to regain a right perspective on life. I remember then that I have no one like you and that you mean more to me than anything the world can offer. Thank you that I belong to you. You take me by the hand, guiding and leading me to a glorious destiny.

*Amen.*

You take me by
the hand guiding
and leading me
into a glorious
destiny

# Psalm 74

*Lord God,*

I belong to you. Help me to remember that your Spirit living in me is greater than the spirit which lives in the world. The enemy of my soul seeks to destroy me. I need you, God. I need you to fight for me and act on my behalf. Instead of looking around me I choose to focus on you. To remember how you have helped me before and remember the promises you have made to me. In you is my victory.

*Amen.*

I need you to
act on my
behalf

# Psalm 75

*Lord God,*

I thank you for your presence in my life. Thank you that you have made your home in me. Sometimes things happen in my life and around me which threaten to shake me. Thank you that you are my firm foundation and I can stand on you. When I start to question your timing and get frustrated by having to wait for you, help me to trust in your plans and trust you will always act at just the right time.

*Amen.*

You are my firm foundation

## About the Author

I live in Eastbourne, in the South East of England. I am married to Jason, we have two adult children, and one dog, Rue.

God has blessed me with a love for His Word, for studying it and sharing it with others. I enjoy teaching from His Word and helping others to see how it relates to their lives in the 21st Century. He has also given me a joy for writing and sharing His Word through my writing.

*If you would like to connect with me, you can do so via:*
- My website: www.vickicottingham.com
- Facebook: @VickiCottinghamWriter
- Instagram: @VickiCottingham

*My other books:*
- Dear Friend...Volume 1 & 2 (Each book has 52 weekly devotions to encourage, challenge and inspire)

- Praying Through Proverbs: Fresh, reflective and helpful everyday prayers inspired from the book of Proverbs
- An Advent Devotional: Hope, Faith, Joy and Love & Worship

These books are all available through Amazon or by contacting me directly.

## About the Illustrator

I live in Eastbourne with my husband, Allen, and my many animals. I am a great animal lover.

I have run a Catholic nursery school for over fifteen years and have always loved using art to illustrate stories for the children and using art for teaching.

If you would like to get in contact with me or would like an individual sketch or commission piece, please email lisasimmonds80@hotmail.com

For my Instagram page please go to pugspraiseandpictures

Printed in Great Britain
by Amazon

71488524R00092